cakes
and pies

Published by:
TRIDENT REFERENCE PUBLISHING
801 12th Avenue South, Suite 400
Naples, Fl 34102 USA

Tel: + 1 (239) 649-7077
www.tridentreference.com
email: sales@tridentreference.com

Cakes and Pies
© TRIDENT REFERENCE PUBLISHING

Publisher
Simon St. John Bailey

Editor-in-chief
Susan Knightley

Prepress
Precision Prep & Press

Includes Index
ISBN 1582797269
UPC 6 15269 97269 4

Printed in The United States

introduction

Baking cakes and pies has never been more fun
than with this selection of tempting recipes.
A bowl, a beater and a few minutes in the kitchen
is all that it takes to fill the house with the homely
warmth and aroma that only a homemade cake
or pie can provide. There's an option on these pages
to please everyone and every occasion. So, discover
the pleasure of trying creative
ideas and watch your friends
and family return for more...

cakes and pies
introduction

Cake-making Hints

- Beating butter or eggs and sugar until fluffy is an important process as little bubbles of air are trapped in the mixture and it is this air which helps to produce a light-textured cake.
- The oven should be preheated to the correct temperature before placing the cake in to cook. Do not open the oven door until at least halfway through the recommended cooking time or the rising process is interrupted.
- Before turning out a cake, loosen it from the sides of the tin with a spatula or palette knife.
- Most undecorated cakes can be frozen successfully, wrapped in freezer wrap or in a freezer bag. To thaw, leave in package and thaw at room temperature for 1-3 hours, according to the size.

Pie-making Secrets

- The best pastry is made using chilled butter and water. Handle the pastry as little as possible, and use only your fingertips for kneading. In hot weather chill the utensils before using.
- Always add liquid cautiously as the amount required can vary depending on the flour that you use.
- When rolling out the pastry, lift and turn to ensure an even thickness.
- Uncooked pastry cases can be frozen for up to 3 months.
- Always preheat the oven before baking pastry.
- To bake blind means to precook the pastry case without the filling. Line the uncooked pastry case with greaseproof paper or a double layer of aluminum foil. Place uncooked rice or dried beans on the paper to weigh down the pastry, as this prevents it from rising during cooking. Make sure that you push the rice or beans right to the sides, to support them. Bake as directed in recipe.
- Allow a cooked filling to cool before putting it into the pie or the pastry will be tough and soggy.

Difficulty scale

■☐☐ I Easy to do

■■☐ I Requires attention

■■■ I Requires experience

glazed
apple cake

a

■ ■ □ | Cooking time: 80 minutes - Preparation time: 15 minutes

method

1. Place butter and sugar in a bowl and beat until light and fluffy. Gradually beat in eggs. Sift flour and baking powder together over butter mixture (a), add milk and vanilla essence and fold into butter mixture.

2. Spoon mixture into a greased and lined 23 cm/9 in round cake tin (b). Arrange apple slices attractively over top of mixture (c) and bake at 160°C/325°F/Gas 3 for 1 hour or until cake is cooked when tested with skewer.

3. To make glaze, place butter, sugar and milk in a saucepan and heat over a low heat, stirring constantly, until sugar dissolves. Bring to the boil, then reduce heat and simmer for 15 minutes or until mixture thickens. Pour hot glaze over hot cake in tin. Cool cake in tin.

Makes a 23 cm/9 in round cake

ingredients

> 185 g/6 oz butter, softened
> 1/2 cup/100 g/3 1/2 oz caster sugar
> 3 eggs, lightly beaten
> 2 1/2 cups/315 g/10 oz flour
> 2 teaspoons baking powder
> 1/4 cup/60 ml/2 fl oz milk
> 1 teaspoon vanilla essence
> 3 apples, peeled, cored and sliced

glaze
> 60 g/2 oz butter
> 3/4 cup/185 g/6 oz sugar
> 1/2 cup/125 ml/4 fl oz milk

tip from the chef

When available, you may want to scatter some fresh blueberries over the apples. A pinch or two of mixed spice can also be added to the glaze if desired.

b

c

strawberry sponge

ingredients
> 3 eggs
> $^1/_2$ cup/100 g/$3^1/_2$ oz caster sugar
> $^1/_4$ cup/30 g/1 oz cornflour
> $^1/_4$ cup/30 g/1 oz plain flour
> $^1/_4$ cup/30 g/1 oz self-raising flour
> 200 g/$6^1/_2$ oz strawberry fromage frais
> 250 g/8 oz strawberries, hulled and halved
> icing sugar

method
1. Place eggs in a bowl and beat with an electric mixer for 5 minutes or until light and fluffy. Gradually add sugar, beating well after each addition until mixture is thick and creamy.
2. Sift together cornflour, plain flour and self-raising flour. Fold flour mixture into egg mixture.
3. Pour batter into two 18 cm/7 in round cake tins lined with nonstick baking paper and bake at 180°C/350°F/Gas 4 for 15 minutes or until cake springs back when lightly pressed with fingertips.
4. Turn cakes onto wire racks to cool. Spread one cake with fromage frais and top with strawberries. Place remaining cake on top, sprinkle with icing sugar and decorate with extra strawberries, if desired.

Serves 12

tip from the chef
When baking, have eggs at room temperature –this will ensure that baked products gain maximum volume.

walnut
banana cake

■□□ | Cooking time: 1 hour - Preparation time: 5 minutes

method

1. Mix all ingredients together in a bowl.
2. Spoon mixture into a greased and lined tin.
3. Bake in moderate oven for 1 hour or until cooked when tested with a skewer.
4. Cool 10 minutes before turning onto wire rack to cool completely.

....

Makes 1 cake

ingredients

> 500 g/1 lb ripe bananas, mashed
> 45 g/1 1/2 oz walnuts, chopped
> 3/4 cup sunflower oil
> 105 g/3 1/2 oz sultanas
> 75 g/2 1/2 oz rolled oats
> 155 g/5 oz wholemeal flour
> 2 teaspoons baking powder
> 1/4 cup sugar

tip from the chef

To test if your cake is cooked, insert a skewer into the thickest part of the cake. If the skewer comes away clean, cake is cooked. If there is still cake mixture on the skewer, cook for 5 minutes longer then test again.

banana
upside-down cake

■□□ | Cooking time: 55 minutes - Preparation time: 10 minutes

ingredients

> **nutty topping**
> - 60 g/2 oz butter
> - 3/4 cup/125 g/4 oz brown sugar
> - 100 g/3 1/2 oz macadamias, roughly chopped
> - 3 bananas, sliced lengthwise

ginger cake
> - 100 g/3 1/2 oz butter, softened
> - 1/2 cup/125 g/4 oz sugar
> - 2 eggs, lightly beaten
> - 2 cups/250 g/8 oz flour
> - 1 teaspoon baking powder
> - 1 teaspoon ground ginger
> - 1/2 cup/125 ml/4 fl oz milk

method

1. To make topping, place butter and brown sugar in a saucepan and cook over a low heat, stirring constantly, until sugar dissolves and mixture thickens to a syrup. Add macadamias.
2. Pour mixture over the base of a greased 23 cm/9 in round cake tin (a). Top with banana slices (b) and set aside.
3. To make cake, place butter and sugar in a bowl and beat until light and fluffy. Gradually beat in eggs. Sift together flour, baking powder and ginger. Fold flour mixture into butter mixture, alternately with milk.
4. Spoon mixture over topping in tin (c) and bake at 180°C/350°F/Gas 4 for 50 minutes or until cake is cooked when tested with a skewer. Stand cake in tin for 5 minutes before turning out. Serve hot or warm.

....
Makes a 23 cm/9 in round cake

tip from the chef

Native to Australia, the macadamia nut has a very hard shell and a delicious rich buttery flavor.

a

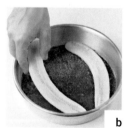

b

c

gingerbread
apricot cake

■□□ I Cooking time: 40 minutes - Preparation time: 10 minutes

method

1. Combine butter and sugar in small bowl, mix until smooth. Spread mixture into a greased and lined 23 cm/9 in tube tin. Sprinkle with pecans and top with apricots.
2. To make gingerbread, place flours, baking powder, ginger, nutmeg and sugar in a large bowl. Combine golden syrup, water and butter in saucepan, stir over low heat until butter is melted. Cool slightly and pour into dry ingredients. Mix until well combined.
3. Spoon gingerbread into prepared tin. Bake at 180°C/350°F/Gas 4 for 35-40 minutes. Stand 15 minutes before turning out onto a wire rack to cool.

....
Serves 10

ingredients

> 1/4 cup butter, softened
> 1/2 cup/100 g/3 1/2 oz brown sugar
> 4 tablespoons chopped pecans
> 1/2 cup dried apricots, soaked

gingerbread

> 1 cup/125 g/4 oz plain flour, sifted
> 1/2 cup/60 g/2 oz self-rising flour, sifted
> 1/2 teaspoon baking powder, sifted
> 3 teaspoons ground ginger
> 1/2 teaspoon ground nutmeg
> 1/2 cup/100 g/ 3 1/2 oz brown sugar
> 1/2 cup golden syrup
> 1/2 cup water
> 1/2 cup butter

tip from the chef

If pecans are unavailable, you can use walnuts instead.

crumble
berry cake

■■□ | Cooking time: 45 minutes - Preparation time: 15 minutes

ingredients

> 60 g/2 oz butter
> 3/4 cup/170 g/51/2 oz caster sugar
> 1 egg
> 1 cup/125 g/4 oz plain flour
> 1 cup/125 g/4 oz self-raising flour
> 1/2 cup/125 ml/4 fl oz milk
> 250 g/8 oz fresh or frozen blackberries or raspberries

topping

> 60 g/2 oz butter
> 1/2 cup/90 g/3 oz brown sugar
> 1/2 cup/60 g/2 oz plain flour
> 1/2 teaspoon ground mixed spice

sauce

> 250 g/8 oz fresh or frozen blackberries or raspberries
> 3 tablespoons caster sugar
> 2 tablespoons lemon juice

method

1. To make topping, place butter, brown sugar, flour and mixed spice in a food processor and process until mixture resembles fine breadcrumbs. Set aside.
2. Place butter and caster sugar in a bowl and beat until light and fluffy. Beat in egg. Sift together plain flour and self-raising flour. Fold flour mixture and milk, alternately, into butter mixture, then stir in berries.
3. Spoon batter into a greased and lined 20 cm/8 in springform tin. Sprinkle cake with topping and bake at 180°C/350°F/Gas 4 for 45 minutes or until cooked when tested with a skewer. Allow cake to cool in tin for 10 minutes before removing to a wire rack to cool completely.
4. To make sauce, place berries, sugar and lemon juice in a food processor or blender and process until smooth. Push sauce through a sieve and discard pips. Serve sauce with cake.

Makes a 20 cm/8 in round cake

tip from the chef
To enrich topping, add 2 tablespoons chopped hazelnuts. Remember not to process mixture too long.

apricot
almond shortcake

■ ■ ■ | Cooking time: 50 minutes - Preparation time: 20 minutes

method

1. Beat butter and sugar until light and creamy. Add egg and beat well, stir in flours. Knead until smooth. Divide pastry into two equal portions; refrigerate for 30 minutes. Roll out each portion to a circle. Press one circle into a greased and lined 20 cm/8 in deep cake tin.

2. To make filling, beat butter, sugar and egg yolk until light and fluffy. Stir in almonds, flour and apricots. Spread over pastry in tin. Place second circle over filling and press edges together. Bake at 180°C/350°F/Gas 4 for 35-40 minutes. Stand 15 minutes and turn out on a wire rack to cool.

3. To make topping, place almonds and sugar in a bowl. Stir in combined egg yolks and amaretto. Set aside one-third of mixture. Add 1 tablespoon unbeaten egg white to remaining mixture and spread over sides and top of shortcake.

4. Add 2 tablespoons egg white to reserved almond mixture and spoon into a piping bag fitted with a star nozzle. Pipe a zigzag pattern over top and small rosettes around the edge. Place cake on a baking tray and bake at 250°C/500°F/Gas 9 for 8-10 minutes or until lightly browned. Spoon two-thirds of jam between zigzag piping and set aside for 10 minutes. Spread sides with remaining jam and coat with almonds. Cool cake completely before cutting.

ingredients

> 125 g/4 oz butter
> 125 g/4 oz sugar
> 1 egg
> 90 g/3 oz self-raising flour, sifted
> 90 g/3 oz plain flour, sifted

filling

> 45 g/1 1/2 oz butter
> 2 tablespoons caster sugar
> 1 egg yolk
> 90 g/3 oz ground almonds
> 2 teaspoons flour
> 440 g/14 oz canned apricots, drained and puréed

topping

> 410 g/13 oz ground almonds
> 5 tablespoons caster sugar
> 6 eggs, separated
> 2 tablespoons amaretto liqueur
> 250 g/8 oz apricot jam, warmed and sieved
> 60 g/2 oz flaked almonds, toasted

....
Serves 8

easter cake

ingredients

> 185 g/6 oz butter, softened
> 3/4 cup/125 g/4 oz brown sugar
> 2 eggs
> 1/3 cup/90 ml/3 fl oz golden syrup
> 1 1/2 cups/185 g/6 oz self-raising flour, sifted
> 1/2 cup/60 g/2 oz plain flour, sifted
> 1 teaspoon ground cinnamon
> 1 teaspoon ground nutmeg
> 3/4 cup/185 ml/6 fl oz milk
> foil wrapped chocolate eggs

method

1. Place butter, sugar, eggs, golden syrup, self-raising flour, plain flour, cinnamon, nutmeg and milk in a bowl and beat for 5 minutes or until mixture is smooth.
2. Pour mixture into a greased 23 cm/9 in fluted ring tin and bake at 180°C/350°F/Gas 4 for 40 minutes or until cake is cooked when tested with a skewer. Stand cake in tin for 5 minutes before turning onto a wire rack to cool.
3. Just prior to serving fill center of cake with chocolate eggs.

Makes a 23 cm/9 in ring cake

tip from the chef

Cool cakes on a wire rack so that the air can circulate freely around them. This prevents cakes getting soggy in the middle and collapsing.

fudge cake

■□□ | Cooking time: 35 minutes - Preparation time: 15 minutes

method

1. Place butter and chocolate in a heatproof bowl set over a saucepan of simmering water and cook, stirring, until melted and combined. Remove from heat and set aside to cool slightly.

2. Place egg yolks and 2/3 cup/140 g/4 1/2 oz sugar in a bowl and beat until light and fluffy. Fold in coffee, hazelnuts and chocolate mixture. Sift together flour and cocoa powder, then fold into mixture.

3. Beat egg whites in a clean bowl until soft peaks form. Gradually add remaining sugar, beating well after each addition until stiff peaks form. Fold egg whites into chocolate mixture.

4. Spoon mixture into a greased and lined deep 23 cm/9 in flan tin and bake at 180°C/350°F/Gas 4 for 30 minutes or until cooked when tested with a skewer. Stand in tin for 5 minutes before turning onto a wire rack to cool completely.

5. To make custard, place egg yolks, sugar and milk in a heatproof bowl and whisk to combine. Place bowl over a saucepan of simmering water and cook, whisking constantly, until mixture thickens. Remove from heat, stir in pistachios and set aside to cool. Serve with cake.

....
Serves 8

ingredients

> **90 g/3 oz butter**
> **90 g/3 oz dark chocolate, chopped**
> **4 eggs, separated**
> **1 cup/220 g/7 oz caster sugar**
> **1/4 cup/60 ml/2 fl oz strong black coffee**
> **60 g/2 oz ground hazelnuts**
> **1/2 cup/60 g/2 oz flour**
> **1/2 cup/45 g/1 1/2 oz cocoa powder**

pistachio custard

> **4 egg yolks, beaten**
> **1/3 cup/75 g/2 1/2 oz caster sugar**
> **1 cup/250 ml/8 fl oz milk**
> **60 g/2 oz chopped pistachios**

tip from the chef

Chocolate melts more rapidly if broken into small pieces. The melting process should occur slowly, as chocolate scorches if overheated.

black
and white cake

ingredients

> 155 g/5 oz butter, melted
> 2 cups/250 g/8 oz
  self-raising flour, sifted
> 1¹/2 cups/330 g/10¹/2 oz
  caster sugar
> ²/3 cup/60 g/2 oz cocoa
  powder, sifted
> 2 eggs
> 1 cup/250 ml/8 fl oz milk
> 8 dark chocolate truffles
> 8 white chocolate truffles

white chocolate glaze

> 185 g/6 oz white
  chocolate, chopped
> ¹/4 cup/60 ml/2 fl oz
  double cream

method

1. Place butter, flour, sugar, cocoa powder, eggs and milk in a bowl and beat until combined.
2. Spoon mixture into a greased 23 cm/9 in fluted ring tin and bake at 180°C/350°F/Gas 4 for 40 minutes or until cooked when tested with a skewer. Allow cake to stand in tin for 10 minutes before turning onto a wire rack to cool completely.
3. To make glaze, place chocolate in a heatproof bowl set over a saucepan of simmering water and heat, stirring until melted. Add cream and stir until smooth.
4. Drizzle glaze over cake, leaving some of the cake exposed to give a black and white effect. Allow glaze to set. Place cake on a serving plate and fill center with truffles.

Makes a 23 cm/9 in ring cake

tip from the chef
For another stylish black and white alternative, drizzle melted dark chocolate over the white chocolate coating after the coating has set.

orange
and lime cake

■□□ | Cooking time: 40 minutes - Preparation time: 10 minutes

method

1. Place butter, lime and orange rinds in a large mixing bowl and beat until light and creamy. Add sugar a little at a time, beating well after each addition. Beat in eggs one at a time and mix well. Fold in flour alternately with yogurt.

2. Spoon mixture into a greased 20 cm/8 in ring tin. Bake at 180°C/350°F/Gas 4 for 30-35 minutes or until cooked. Stand in tin for 5 minutes, then turn out on a wire rack with a tray underneath.

3. To make syrup, place lime juice, orange juice and sugar in a saucepan. Cook over a medium heat, stirring constantly, until sugar dissolves. Bring mixture to the boil, without stirring, and boil for 3 minutes. Remove from heat and pour hot syrup over hot cake. Set aside to cool.

ingredients

> 125 g/4 oz butter
> 1 teaspoon grated lime rind
> 3 teaspoons grated orange rind
> 220 g/7 oz caster sugar
> 3 eggs
> 200 g/6½ oz self-raising flour, sifted
> 125 g/4 oz natural yogurt

syrup

> 2 tablespoons lime juice
> 3 tablespoons orange juice
> 3 tablespoons sugar

Serves 10

tip from the chef

When grating lime and orange rind use only the external part, as the interior white pith will give the pie a bitter taste.

rum
coconut cake

■■□ | Cooking time: 75 minutes - Preparation time: 20 minutes

method

1. Sift flour and baking powder together into a bowl. Add coconut and sugar and mix to combine. Place eggs, yogurt and milk in a bowl and whisk to combine. Add to dry ingredients and mix until smooth.
2. Spoon batter into a greased and lined 23 cm/9 in round cake tin and bake at 180°C/350°F/Gas 4 for 1 hour or until cooked when tested with a skewer.
3. To make syrup, place sugar, water and rum in a saucepan and cook over a low heat, stirring constantly, for 4-5 minutes or until sugar dissolves. Bring to the boil, then reduce heat and simmer for 4 minutes or until syrup thickens slightly. Pour half the hot syrup over hot cake in tin. Stand cake in tin for 5 minutes before turning onto a serving platter. Serve with remaining syrup and golden bananas.
4. Place bananas, butter, sugar, rum and lime juice in a frying pan. Cook over a high heat, turning bananas several times, for 5 minutes or until bananas and syrup are golden.

....
Makes a 23 cm/9 in round cake

ingredients

> 1 1/2 cups/185 g/6 oz self-raising flour
> 1/2 teaspoon baking powder
> 60 g/2 oz shredded coconut
> 1 cup/220 g/7 oz caster sugar
> 2 eggs, lightly beaten
> 1 cup/200 g/6 1/2 oz natural yogurt
> 1 cup/250 ml/8 fl oz milk

rum syrup

> 1 cup/220 g/7 oz caster sugar
> 3/4 cup/185 ml/6 fl oz water
> 1/4 cup/60 ml/2 fl oz coconut-flavored rum

golden bananas

> 6 bananas, halved lengthwise
> 60 g/2 oz butter, melted
> 1/4 cup/45 g/1 1/2 oz brown sugar
> 1/4 cup/60 ml/2 fl oz dark rum
> 1 tablespoon lime juice

ip from the chef

f coconut-flavored rum is unavailable, *range-flavored liqueur is a suitable* *ubstitute.*

lemon
sultana cheesecake

■ ■ □ I Cooking time: 40 minutes - Preparation time: 15 minutes

ingredients

pastry
> 1/2 cup/60 g/2 oz flour
> 1/4 cup/30 g/1 oz cornflour
> 1/4 cup/30 g/1 oz custard powder
> 4 teaspoons icing sugar
> 60 g/2 oz butter
> 1 egg yolk

filling
> 375 g/12 oz cream cheese, softened
> 1/4 cup/45 g/1 1/2 oz natural yogurt
> 1/2 cup/100 g/3 1/2 oz caster sugar
> 2 eggs
> 1 teaspoon vanilla essence
> 2 teaspoons finely grated lemon rind
> 170 g/5 1/2 oz sultanas

lemon topping
> 1/2 cup/125 ml/4 fl oz double cream
> 2 teaspoons lemon juice
> 1/2 teaspoon finely grated lemon rind

method

1. To make pastry, sift together flour, cornflour, custard powder and icing sugar into a large mixing bowl. Rub in butter with fingertips until mixture resembles coarse breadcrumbs. Stir in egg yolk and enough water to make a firm dough. Wrap in plastic food wrap and refrigerate for 30 minutes.
2. Roll out pastry to fit the base of a greased 20 cm/8 in springform tin. Prick pastry with a fork and bake at 220°C/425°F/Gas 7 for 10 minutes. Set aside to cool.
3. To make filling, beat cream cheese, yogurt, sugar, eggs, vanilla and lemon rind in a mixing bowl until smooth. Fold in sultanas. Spoon mixture over pastry in tin. Reduce oven temperature to 180°C/350°F/Gas 4 and bake for 20-25 minutes or until firm. Turn off oven and leave cheesecake to cool in oven with door ajar.
4. To make topping, place cream, lemon juice and rind in a small saucepan and bring to simmering, then simmer, stirring, for 5 minutes or until mixture thickens. Pour topping over cooled cheesecake and chill until required.

....
Serves 8

tip from the chef

The tangy taste of lemon combines with cream cheese and yogurt to make this irresistible cheesecake.

classic
baked cheesecake

■□□ | Cooking time: 1 hour - Preparation time: 15 minutes

method

1. To make base, place biscuits and butter in a bowl and mix to combine (a). Press mixture over the base of a greased and lined 23 cm/9 in springform tin.
2. To make filling, place cream cheese and sugar in a bowl and beat until smooth. Add eggs one by one (b). Then beat in sour cream, cream and lemon juice. Fold in flour.
3. Pour filling over base (c). Bake at 160°C/325°F/Gas 3 for 1 hour or until firm. Cool cheesecake in tin.

Makes a 23 cm/9 in round cake

ingredients

base
> 125 g/4 oz sweet biscuits, crushed
> 30 g/1 oz butter, melted

filling
> 440 g/14 oz cream cheese, softened
> 1 cup/220 g/7 oz caster sugar
> 4 eggs
> 155 g/5 oz sour cream
> 1/2 cup/125 ml/4 fl oz double cream
> 2 tablespoons lemon juice
> 1/3 cup/45 g/1 1/2 oz flour, sifted

tip from the chef

For a simple decoration, spread the top of this traditional cheesecake with thick sour cream. Sprinkle with freshly grated nutmeg and garnish with a few berries.

a

b

c

pistachio
cheesecake

■ ■ □ | Cooking time: 45 minutes - Preparation time: 15 minutes

method

1. Place walnuts, 90 g/3 oz pistachios and brown sugar in a bowl and mix to combine. Set aside.

2. Cut ten 20 cm/8 in circles from filo pastry. Place one circle of pastry in a greased and lined 20 cm/8 in round sandwich tin, brush with butter and sprinkle with nut mixture. Repeat layers to use half the pastry and half the nut mixture. In a second greased and lined 20 cm/8 in round sandwich tin layer the remaining pastry and nut mixture in the same way. Bake pastry stacks at 180°C/350°F/Gas 4 for 30 minutes or until golden.

3. To make syrup, place sugar and water in a saucepan and heat, stirring constantly, over a medium heat until sugar dissolves. Bring to simmering and simmer for 10 minutes or until syrup thickens. Pour hot syrup over hot pastry in tin. Cool in tin.

4. Place ricotta cheese and rosewater in a bowl and beat to combine. Spread half the mixture over one pastry stack. Top with other pastry stack, spread with remaining ricotta mixture and sprinkle with remaining pistachios.

....

Serves 8

ingredients

> 90 g/3 oz chopped walnuts
> 185 g/6 oz chopped pistachios
> 1 cup/170 g/5^1/$_2$ oz brown sugar
> 375 g/12 oz filo pastry
> 125 g/4 oz butter, melted
> 250 g/8 oz ricotta cheese
> 1 teaspoon rosewater

syrup

> 2 cups/440 g/14 oz caster sugar
> 1 cup/250 ml/8 fl oz water

tip from the chef

Rosewater is an essential ingredient in Middle Eastern and Indian cooking and is used in both savory and sweet dishes. It became fashionable as a flavoring in England during the 16th century and remained a staple ingredient until Victorian times. Rosewater is available from Middle Eastern and Indian food shops and some pharmacies.

chocolate
pecan cheesecake

■□□ | Cooking time: 90 minutes - Preparation time: 15 minutes

method

1. To make base, combine biscuits and butter in a bowl and mix well. Press over the base and sides of a greased 20 cm/8 in springform tin. Refrigerate until firm.
2. To make filling, beat cream cheese, ricotta and sugar until sugar dissolves. Add eggs one at a time, beating well after each addition. Fold in flour and then vanilla essence, cream, chocolate and pecans.
3. Pour mixture into base in tin and bake at 120°C/250°F/Gas 1 for 1¹/₂ hours or until just firm in the center. Turn oven off and cool cheesecake in oven with door ajar. Refrigerate for several hours or overnight before serving.

....
Serves 8

ingredients

base
> 200 g/6¹/₂ oz chocolate biscuits, crushed
> 125 g/4 oz butter, melted

filling
> 1 cup/250 g/8 oz cream cheese
> 1 cup/250 g/8 oz ricotta cheese
> ²/₃ cup/170 g/5¹/₂ oz caster sugar
> 3 eggs
> 3 tablespoons flour, sifted
> 1 teaspoon vanilla essence
> ³/₄ cup/180 ml/6 fl oz thickened cream
> 150 g/5 oz dark chocolate, melted
> 100 g/3¹/₂ oz pecans, chopped

tip from the chef

The berry sauce on page 16 is also suitable to serve with this cheesecake.

almond
ricotta cheesecake

■□□ | Cooking time: 35 minutes - Preparation time: 15 minutes

method

1. To make pastry, place flour in a bowl and rub in butter, using the fingertips, until mixture resembles fine breadcrumbs. Using a knife, mix in egg yolk and water to form a firm dough. Wrap in plastic food wrap and chill for 1 hour. Roll out pastry and line a 23 cm/9 in springform tin. Trim edges.

2. To make filling, combine ricotta, sugar, almonds and lemon rind in a bowl. Beat in vanilla and eggs one at a time.

3. Spoon filling into pastry in tin and bake at 200°C/400°F/Gas 6 for 5 minutes. Reduce heat to 180°C/350°F/Gas 4 and bake for 30 minutes longer, or until filling is firm.

4. To make topping, whip cream and amaretto together until soft peaks form. Just prior to serving turn out cake and spread with topping.

ingredients

pastry

> 250 g/8 oz flour, sifted
> 125 g/4 oz butter
> 1 egg yolk
> 1 tablespoon iced water

filling

> 750 g/1 1/2 lb ricotta cheese
> 125 g/4 oz sugar
> 90 g/3 oz ground almonds
> 1 teaspoon grated lemon rind
> 1/2 teaspoon vanilla essence
> 4 eggs

topping

> 250 ml/8 fl oz cream
> 1 tablespoon amaretto liqueur

....
Serves 8

tip from the chef

A light baked cheesecake that can be served warm or chilled. This cake looks great decorated with chocolate leaves.

carrot
cake with lemon frosting

■□□ | Cooking time: 40 minutes - Preparation time: 15 minutes

method
1. Sift together flour, baking powder and bicarbonate of soda into a bowl, add sugar and mix to combine. Add carrot, pineapple, eggs, oil and cinnamon and mix well (a).
2. Spoon batter into a lined 18 cm/7 in round cake tin (b) and bake at 180°C/350°F/Gas 4 for 35-40 minutes or until cooked when tested with a skewer. Stand cake in tin for 5 minutes before turning onto a wire rack to cool completely.
3. To make frosting, place ricotta cheese, icing sugar and lemon juice in a food processor (c) and process until smooth. Spread over the top of cold cake.

....
Serves 12

ingredients
> 1 cup/125 g/4 oz flour
> 1 teaspoon baking powder
> 1/2 teaspoon bicarbonate of soda
> 3/4 cup/125 g/4 oz brown sugar
> 1 carrot, grated
> 1/2 cup/90 g/3 oz canned pineapple, drained and chopped
> 2 eggs
> 2 tablespoons oil
> 1 teaspoon ground cinnamon

lemon frosting
> 125 g/4 oz ricotta cheese
> 1/4 cup/45 g/1 1/2 oz icing sugar
> 1 tablespoon lemon juice

tip from the chef
To enhance flavor, you may add 1 teaspoon vanilla essence to the topping.
In season, use ripe fresh instead of canned pineapple.

a

b

c

hazelnut
beetroot cake

■□□ | Cooking time: 75 minutes - Preparation time: 10 minutes

method

1. Place butter and sugar in a bowl and beat until light and fluffy. Gradually beat in eggs.
2. Fold beetroot, hazelnuts, flour and orange rind into butter mixture.
3. Spoon mixture into a greased and lined 20 cm/8 in square cake tin and bake at 140°C/275°F/Gas 1 for 1¼ hours or until cake is cooked when tested with a skewer.
4. Stand cake in tin for 5 minutes before turning onto a wire rack to cool. Just prior to serving dust with icing sugar.

ingredients

> 250 g/8 oz butter, softened
> 1 cup/250 g/8 oz sugar
> 4 eggs, lightly beaten
> 185 g/6 oz raw beetroot, finely grated
> 200 g/6½ oz hazelnuts, roasted and ground
> 2½ cups/315 g/10 oz self-raising flour, sifted
> 1 tablespoon finely grated orange rind
> icing sugar, sifted

Makes a 20 cm/8 in square cake

tip from the chef

You can bake this mixture in a loaf tin, then slice and store individual servings. To freeze, wrap portions in freezer wrap and seal. To thaw, leave portion in its wrapping and stand at room temperature for about 30 minutes.

raspberry
mousse flan

■■□ | Cooking time: 20 minutes - Preparation time: 20 minutes

method

1. To make pastry, combine flour, sugar and almonds in a food processor. Add butter and process until mixture resembles fine breadcrumbs. With machine running add egg yolk and enough iced water to form a soft dough. Knead lightly on a floured surface. Wrap in plastic food wrap and refrigerate for 30 minutes.

2. Roll out pastry and line a lightly greased, deep 20 cm/8 in fluted flan tin with a removable base. Refrigerate for 15 minutes. Bake blind at 200°C/400°F/Gas 6 for 10 minutes. Remove weights and cook for 10 minutes longer or until lightly browned.

3. To make filling, beat egg yolks and sugar in a bowl until thick and creamy. Beat egg whites in a separate bowl until stiff peaks form. Fold cream and egg whites into the egg yolk mixture. Then fold 4 tablespoons of egg mixture into raspberry purée. Fold half the gelatin into the raspberry mixture and the remainder into the egg mixture.

4. Place large spoonfuls of egg mixture into pastry case, then top with small spoonfuls of raspberry mixture. Repeat until both mixtures are used. Swirl the mixtures with a skewer. Refrigerate for 2 hours or until firm. Just prior to serving, top with berries.

....
Serves 8

ingredients

almond pastry

> 1¼ cups/155 g/5 oz flour
> 2 tablespoons caster sugar
> 15 g/½ oz ground almonds
> 125 g/4 oz butter, cut into pieces
> 1 egg yolk, lightly beaten

filling

> 2 eggs, separated
> ¼ cup/60 g/2 oz caster sugar
> ½ cup/125 ml/4 fl oz double cream, whipped
> 90 g/3 oz raspberries, puréed
> 8 teaspoons gelatin dissolved in ½ cup/ 125 ml/4 fl oz hot water, cooled
> 500 g/1 lb mixed berries

tip from the chef

Almonds come in two types, bitter and sweet. Bitter, contain prussic acid, a poison that must be leached by heating, and they are used almost exclusively for oils and extracts. Sweet, are the familiar ones used for eating.

rum fig tart

ingredients

pastry
> 1 1/2 cups flour
> 90 g/3 oz butter, cut into small cubes
> 1 egg
> 1 tablespoon sugar
> 2 tablespoons chilled white wine

filling
> 15-20 glacé figs
> 3 tablespoons fig jam
> 1/3 cup rum

method

1. To make pastry, a large bowl combine flour and butter, mix with fingertips until mixture resembles fine breadcrumbs. Add egg, sugar and wine, mix to a soft dough. Knead on lightly floured surface until smooth.
2. Turn onto a lightly floured surface, roll out pastry to fit a 23 cm/9 in flan tin. Bake pastry blind in a hot oven for 10 minutes. Remove pastry weights and cook for a further 10 minutes in moderate oven.
3. To make filling, arrange figs around base of pastry case.
   In a small saucepan heat jam with rum until thin and syrupy. Brush figs with syrup and serve with whipped cream if desired.

....

Serves 8

tip from the chef
If you wish, serve each slice with whipped cream or a scoop of vanilla ice cream.

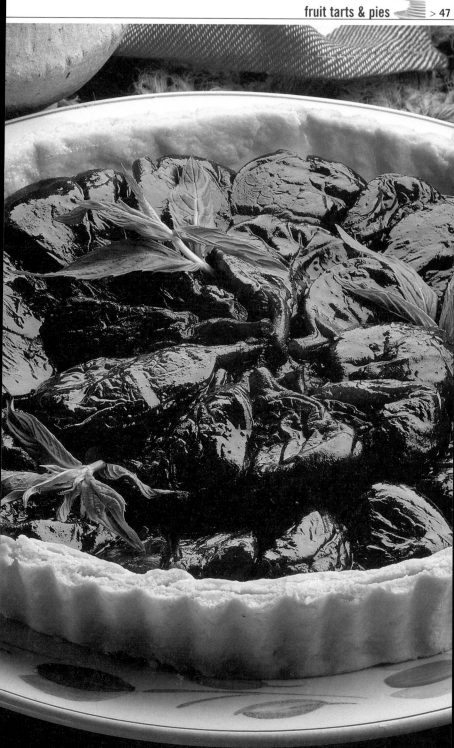

folded
peach and berry pie

■□□ I Cooking time: 30 minutes - Preparation time: 15 minutes

method

1. To make pastry, place flour, butter and sugar in a food processor and process until mixture resembles fine breadcrumbs. With machine running, slowly add enough iced water to form a rough dough. Turn dough on a lightly floured surface and knead until smooth. Wrap in plastic food wrap and chill for 30 minutes.
2. Roll out pastry on a lightly floured surface to form a rough 38 cm/15 in circle. Place pastry in a 23 cm/9 in pie plate or flan tin and allow excess to hang over the sides.
3. To make filling, place peaches, berries, flour and sugar in a bowl and toss to combine. Spoon fruit mixture into pastry case, then fold excess pastry over fruit. Chill pie for 30 minutes.
4. Brush pastry with milk, sprinkle with extra sugar and bake at 190°C/375°F/Gas 5 for 30 minutes or until pastry is cooked and golden.

ingredients

pastry

> **2 cups/250 g/8 oz flour**
> **125 g/4 oz butter, diced**
> **2 tablespoons caster sugar**

filling

> **4 peaches, sliced**
> **375 g/12 oz mixed berries**
> **2 tablespoons flour**
> **1 tablespoon sugar**
> **milk for brushing**
> **extra sugar**

....
Serves 8

tip from the chef

Serve with ice cream or thick cream.

apple
and apricot torte

ingredients

pastry
> 3 cups/375 g/12 oz self-rising flour, sifted
> 1 cup/250 g/8 oz butter
> 1/4 cup/60 ml/2 fl oz water

filling
> 440 g/14 oz canned apple slices, drained
> 440 g/14 oz canned apricot halves, drained
> 3/4 cup/125 g/4 oz golden raisins
> 2-3 tablespoons sugar

method

1. To make pastry, place flour in a bowl, rub in butter with fingertips until mixture resembles fine breadcrumbs. Remove one-third of mixture and set aside. Add enough water to remaining mixture to form a firm dough. Roll out pastry and line the base and sides of a greased 20 cm/8 in springformtin.
2. To make filling, combine apples, apricots and raisins in a bowl. Spoon into pastry case.
3. Mix sugar into reserved pastry crumbs and sprinkle over fruit. Bake at 190°C/375°F/Gas 5 for 10 minutes, reduce oven temperature to 180°C/350°F/Gas 4 and bake for 20 minutes longer or until golden brown.

Serves 4

tip from the chef
Apricots can be replaced by peaches; if so, it is advisable to divide each half into 3 or 4 wedges.

fruit
mince flan

■■□ | Cooking time: 35 minutes - Preparation time: 15 minutes

method

1. To make pastry, sift flour and icing sugar into a bowl, rub in butter. Add egg yolk and enough water to make ingredients cling together. Knead on lightly floured surface until smooth.
2. Roll out to fit a 23 cm/9 in flan tin, trim edges. Bake pastry blind in a moderately hot oven for 10 minutes. Remove pastry weights and cook for a further 10 minutes or until golden brown, cool.
3. To make filling, combine fruit mince, sultanas, breadcrumbs and brandy, spread over pastry case.
4. Place apples and water in a small saucepan, cover and simmer until just tender, drain. Lay apple slices around edge of flan. Bake in moderate oven for 10 minutes, cool.
5. Beat cream until soft peaks form, pipe around edge of flan, dust with cinnamon.

....
Serves 8

ingredients

pastry
> 1¹/₂ cups flour
> 2 tablespoons icing sugar
> 125 g/4 oz butter
> 1 egg yolk

filling
> 410 g/13 oz fruit mince
> ¹/₂ cup sultanas
> ¹/₂ cup fresh breadcrumbs
> 2 tablespoons brandy
> 2 green apples, cored, peeled and thinly sliced
> ¹/₂ cup water
> ³/₄ cup thickened cream
> ground cinnamon

tip from the chef
To make fresh breadcrumbs, process slices of bread, crust removed, for a few seconds.

tangy orange tart

■■□ | Cooking time: 25 minutes - Preparation time: 15 minutes

ingredients

pastry
> 1¹/2 cups flour
> 1 tablespoon caster sugar
> 125 g/4 oz butter, cut into small cubes
> 3 tablespoons orange juice

filling
> 3 tablespoons grated orange rind
> 1¹/2 tablespoons grated lemon rind
> ³/4 cup sugar
> ²/3 cup fresh lime juice
> ¹/3 cup fresh orange juice
> 6 egg yolks
> 4 eggs
> 250 g/8 oz butter, cut into pieces
> ¹/2 cup orange marmalade
> 2 oranges, peeled and sliced

method

1. To make pastry, combine flour, sugar and butter in a food processor until mixture resembles breadcrumbs. Add orange juice, more or less as needed to form a dough (a). Transfer to a bowl, cover and chill for 30 minutes.

2. Roll out pastry to fit a 23 cm/9 in flan tin. Bake blind in a moderately hot oven for 10 minutes. Remove pastry weights and cook for a further 10 minutes.

3. To make filling, combine orange and lemon rind with sugar in a heatproof bowl set over a saucepan of simmering water. Whisk in lime juice, orange juice, egg yolks and eggs. Whisk over medium heat until mixture begins to thicken, do not boil. Gradually whisk in butter (b) and continue to whisk until mixture thickens to a curd, about 2 minutes. Pour mixture into another bowl, cover with plastic wrap and refrigerate until cool.

4. Brush the inside of pastry case with half of the marmalade. Pour filling into pastry case and arrange orange slices on top. Melt remaining marmalade in a small saucepan over low heat and brush the top of the tart (c).

....
Serves 8

tip from the chef
Another delicious option consists in replacing orange slices for a meringue topping and browning under the grill.

a

b

c

cherry tart

■■□ I Cooking time: 30 minutes - Preparation time: 20 minutes

method

1. To make pastry, combine flour and sugar in a bowl and make a well in the center. Add butter, milk, lemon rind and egg yolks and mix, using a knife. Knead lightly until smooth, wrap in plastic food wrap and refrigerate for 30 minutes.
2. Roll out two-thirds of pastry, between two sheets of plastic food wrap, into a rectangle 1 cm/1/2 in thick. Line a greased 10 x 35 cm/4 x 14 in tin with pastry.
3. To make filling, arrange cherries in rows on pastry. Place remaining dough into a piping bag fitted with a plain nozzle and pipe over cherries in a lattice pattern. Pinch edges of pastry strips and base together.
4. Bake at 180°C/350°F/Gas 4 for 25-30 minutes or until golden. Brush warm tart with jam and serve warm or chilled.

....
Serves 8

ingredients

pastry

> 250 g/8 oz flour, sifted
> 125 g/4 oz sugar
> 125 g/4 oz butter, melted and cooled
> 2 tablespoons milk
> 1 teaspoon grated lemon rind
> 2 egg yolks, lightly beaten

filling

> 2 x 440 g/14 oz canned cherries, drained
> 125 g/4 oz peach or apricot jam, warmed and sieved

tip from the chef

This tart is equally as good made using any preserved fruit. You might like to try using peaches, apricots or pears.

rhubarb
and apple tart

▪▪☐ | Cooking time: 75 minutes - Preparation time: 20 minutes

method

1. To make pastry, place flour and icing sugar in a bowl and rub in butter, using your fingertips, until mixture resembles coarse breadcrumbs. Add water and knead to a smooth dough. Wrap in plastic food wrap and refrigerate for 30 minutes.
2. Roll out pastry on a lightly floured surface and line a greased 23 cm/9 in fluted flan tin with a removable base. Bake pastry blind at 200°C/400°F/Gas 6 for 15 minutes. Remove pastry weights and cook for 5 minutes longer.
3. To make filling, poach or microwave rhubarb until tender. Drain well, stir in sugar and set aside to cool. Melt butter in a frying pan and cook apples for 3-4 minutes. Remove apples from pan and set aside to cool. Place cream cheese, sugar, vanilla essence and egg in a bowl and beat until smooth.
4. Spoon rhubarb into pastry case, then top with cream cheese mixture and arrange apple slices attractively on the top. Reduce oven temperature to 180°C/350°F/Gas 4 and cook for 40-45 minutes or until filling is firm.

....
Serves 10

ingredients

pastry

> 1 cup/125 g/4 oz flour, sifted
> 2 teaspoons icing sugar, sifted
> 90 g/3 oz butter, cubed
> 4 teaspoons iced water

filling

> 6 stalks rhubarb, chopped
> 2 tablespoons sugar
> 30 g/1 oz butter
> 3 green apples, cored, peeled and sliced
> 125 g/4 oz cream cheese
> 1/3 cup/90 g/3 oz sugar
> 1 teaspoon vanilla essence
> 1 egg

tip from the chef

The pastry for this tart can be made in a food processor if you wish. Process flour, icing sugar and butter until mixture resembles coarse breadcrumbs. With machine running add water and continue to process until a smooth dough forms.

pecan tart

■□□ | Cooking time: 40 minutes - Preparation time: 10 minutes

method

1. To make filling, beat butter, sugar and vanilla essence until light and fluffy. Add eggs one at a time, beating well after each addition. Fold in molasses, flour, spices and pecans.

2. Spoon filling into pastry case and bake at 160°C/325°F/Gas 3 for 35-40 minutes or until firm and golden.

....

Serves 4

ingredients

> 1 x 18 cm/7 in unbaked shortcrust pastry case

filling

> 30 g/1 oz butter
> 1/4 cup/45 g/11/2 oz brown sugar
> 1 teaspoon vanilla essence
> 2 eggs
> 1/3 cup/125 g/4 oz molasses
> 4 teaspoons flour, sifted
> 1 teaspoon ground pumpkin pie spice
> 1 teaspoon ground cinnamon
> 3/4 cup/90 g/3 oz pecans, roughly chopped

tip from the chef

Any of the pastry recipes in this book is suitable for this tart.

coffee
nut pie

■□□ | Cooking time: 5 minutes - Preparation time: 15 minutes

method

1. To make base, place biscuits and butter in a bowl and mix well to combine. Press biscuit mixture into a 23 cm/9 in flan tin with a removable base.
2. To make filling, place ice cream and coffee mixture in a bowl and mix to combine. Spoon over base in tin and place in freezer.
3. To make topping, place milk, sugar and chocolate in a saucepan and cook over a low heat, stirring, until chocolate is melted and mixture is smooth. Stir in pecans or walnuts, allow to cool, then pour topping over filling and freeze until firm.

....
Serves 6

ingredients

base

> 220 g/7 oz chocolate biscuits, crushed
> 125 g/4 oz butter

filling

> 1 liter/1³/4 pt vanilla ice cream, softened
> 2 teaspoons instant coffee dissolved in 4 teaspoons hot water, cooled

topping

> ¹/2 cup/125 ml/4 fl oz evaporated milk
> ¹/2 cup/100 g/3¹/2 oz caster sugar
> 200 g/6¹/2 oz dark chocolate
> 60 g/2 oz pecans or walnuts, chopped

tip from the chef

This version of the traditional American Mud Pie is sure to be popular as a dessert or as a special afternoon tea treat. Decorating suggestion: top with chocolate caraques and whipped cream.

index